Rookie
Read-About® Holidays

100th Day
of School

By Melissa Schiller

Consultant
Don L. Curry
Reading and Content Consultant

Children's Press®
A Division of Scholastic Inc.
New York Toronto London Auckland Sydney
Mexico City New Delhi Hong Kong
Danbury, Connecticut

Designer: Herman Adler Design
Photo Researcher: Caroline Anderson
The photo on the cover shows three children in 100th Day hats.

Library of Congress Cataloging-in-Publication Data

Schiller, Melissa.
  100th day of school / by Melissa Schiller ; consultant, Don Curry.
    p. cm. – (Rookie read-about holidays)
Includes index.
Summary: Describes ways of celebrating the one hundredth day of school,
such as making hats with one hundred stickers, being quiet for one
hundred seconds, and recycling one hundred cans.
  ISBN 0-516-25856-7 (lib. bdg.)   0-516-27943-2 (pbk.)
  1. Hundred (The number)–Juvenile literature. 2. Special
days–Juvenile literature. [1. Hundred (The number) 2. Special days.]
I. Title: One hundredth day of school. II. Title. III. Series.
  QA141.15.S32 2003
  513.2'11–dc21
                              2003000463

    6 7 8 9 10 R 12 11 10 09 08 07 06

Today is the 100th day of school!

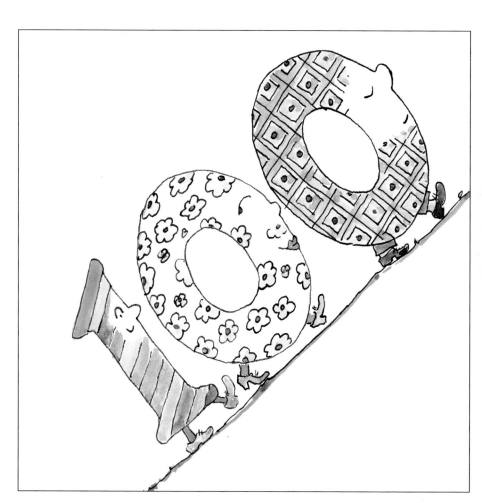

We have been counting since the first day of school. Today we will celebrate (SEL-uh-brate).

5

We make hats for the special day. We use paper, scissors, and stickers. Each hat has 100 stickers on it.

We put our handprints on a banner. There are 100 handprints. Can you count them?

9

We put 100 pieces of
cereal on a string to make
a necklace (NEK-liss).

We made a paper chain
to hang around the room.
There are 10 colors. Can
you name them?

We tell 100 jokes.
We laugh a lot.

We count 100 cubes (kyoobs). Then we use a ruler to see how long they are.

We did not talk for 100 seconds! We looked at the clock. It was hard to be so quiet.

We recycle (ree-SYE-kuhl) 100 cans.

How many jumping jacks
can you do in 100 seconds?
Can you hop on one foot
100 times?

Touch your toes 100 times!

Here is a puzzle with 100 pieces. We work to put it all together.

23

We make 100 paper airplanes. We test which ones can fly the farthest.

When we count to 100,
we make groups of 10.
In each bag there are:

 10 beads

 10 snacks

 10 balls

 10 feathers

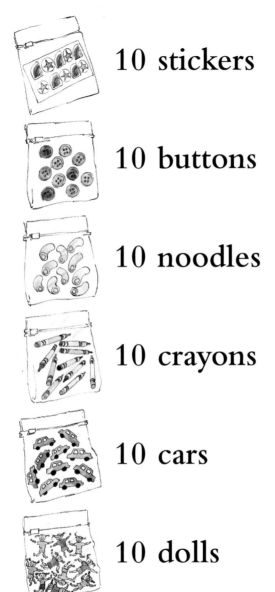

10 stickers

10 buttons

10 noodles

10 crayons

10 cars

10 dolls

Now it is time for a parade. We put on our hats. We shout and smile as we celebrate our 100th day.

How do you celebrate the
100th day of school?

Words You Know

cereal

cubes

handprints

paper hats

parade

puzzle

recycle

Index

About the Author

Melissa Schiller taught elementary school for five years and has written a number of children's books. She lives in New York City and has two sons, ages two and four, who are her inspiration for writing.

Photo Credits

Photographs © 2003: Corbis Images: 24 (Stephen S.T. Bradley), 11 (Jose Luis Pelaez, Inc.); Dubuque Community Schools/Gary Olsen: cover, 6; Ellen B. Senisi: 15, 30 top right; PhotoDisc/Getty Images/Andersen Ross: 16; PhotoEdit/David Young-Wolff: 10, 30 top left; Stock Boston: 9, 30 bottom left (Bob Daemmrich), 12 (Gregg Mancuso), 28, 31 top (Lawrence Migdale); The Image Bank/Getty Images/David Zelick: 29; The Image Works: 23, 31 bottom left (Elizabeth Crews), 19, 20, 21, 31 bottom right (Bob Daemmrich).

Illustrations by Paul Rowntree